UNWRITTEN

THE LEADERSHIP PLAN NO ONE GAVE YOU—
UNTIL NOW

MELANIE MATTA

PRINCIPAL PRINCIPLES PUBLICATIONS
UNITED STATES OF AMERICA

Melanie Matta/Principal Principles Publications
www.edleadershiplab.com
melaniermatta@gmail.com

Ordering Information:
Quantity sales. Special discounts are available on quantity purchases by corporations, associations, and others. For details, contact the "Special Sales Department" at the address above.

Unwritten/ Melanie Matta. —1st ed.
ISBN 979-8-9987351-7-2

Table of Contents

Acknowledgments

To every school leader who's ever felt alone or unseen — this book is for you. Your courage and heart keep schools alive.

To the students, staff, families, and board members of Hope Elementary — thank you for allowing us to do what's possible when a school is built on trust and love.

To my mentors Janet Jones and Nicole Glentzer — thank you for shaping how I lead. Every lesson, especially the hard ones...mattered.

To my family — thank you for being my constant cheerleaders.

To Cohort 1 and Powerhouse — you are the proof that leadership doesn't have to be lonely when you choose to walk it alongside others.

And to you, the reader — thank you for leading differently. Our kids and our world are better because of you.

Lead boldly. Lead human.

—Melanie Matta

The Gap

You've done the training. You've earned the title. You've prepared for the role.

And yet, on day one, you're handed the keys and expected to lead a community of humans through complexity, uncertainty, and change... with no real roadmap.

That's the gap. The one no credential program warns you about.

Because educational leadership isn't just about managing systems.

It's about navigating trust, tension, culture, and connection—all in real time.

This book was written to close that gap.

Unwritten: The Leadership Plan No One Gives You— *Until Now* isn't a checklist. It's not a theoretical framework. It's the human blueprint for leading real people through real challenges in real schools. It's the guide I needed but never received.

When I stepped into my role as Superintendent/Principal of a small, rural district, I didn't inherit a blank slate; I inherited broken trust, institutional fatigue, and a staff unsure whether to hope again. No textbook covered what to do when systems fail, when silence masks trauma, or when your presence matters more than your plan.

And yet, not all leadership transitions begin in crisis.

Some leaders walk into schools that are steady, thriving, and deeply rooted in the community. That is a gift... and a responsibility. Even in strong systems, the work of leadership remains deeply human. Preserving a healthy culture, honoring a predecessor's legacy, and guiding people through inevitable change still requires intentionality, trust-building, and the ability to lead without ego.

Whether you're rebuilding something broken or continuing something beautiful, one truth holds:

Leadership doesn't begin with strategy—it begins with how you show up.

Inside this book, you'll find the tools, mindsets, and real-world practices that too often go untaught:

- How to read invisible data and spot the patterns that silently shape culture

- How to rebuild trust you didn't break or be a good steward of trust you've been gifted

- How to lead change without losing yourself

- How to respond when resistance isn't just professional, it's personal

You'll also gain access to **The Innovative Leader's 90-Day Entry Plan**, a practical, field-tested framework built through my work with EdLeadership Lab. Visit Edleadershiplab.com/store and apply the discount code *UNWRITTEN* at checkout.

This plan is designed to help leaders slow down, listen deeply, build trust, and diagnose systems before designing solutions. It's not about looking impressive... It's about leading with presence and purpose.

This is a book for the leader who's ready to do the real work—the human work.

No one expects you to have all the answers, but they do need you to be real.

You just have to begin with courage, clarity, and a willingness to lead differently.

Take a breath. Turn the page.

Let's rewrite the story of school leadership—*together.*

PART 1

Before You Begin

Why this book matters—and why the work begins with YOU.

When I stepped into my role as Superintendent/Principal of a small, rural school district, I walked into chaos. The district was deeply dysfunctional. Computers had been wiped. Files were gone. Trust was shattered. I didn't feel like I was being handed a leadership opportunity, but more so the remnants of an organization on life support.

No one prepared me for that.

There wasn't a course in my credential program titled "What to Do When the Entire System is Broken." There was no playbook for earning trust from a team that had been burned by leadership. No training on how to rebuild when all you inherit is silence, side-eyes, and surface-level compliance.

But this is the real work. This is the part no one gives you.

This book exists because you deserve better.

Unwritten is the leadership plan I wish someone had handed me. Not a script. Not a checklist. A guide. A mindset. A blueprint that helps you enter a school or district with humility, clarity, and the tools to lead like a human first.

Systems are important, but people matter more in leadership. They don't teach you how to lead people when you're also navigating board meetings, special ed compliance, kitchen equipment failures, bus driver shortages, and family trauma all in the same week.

When you lead a school, especially in small systems, you are expected to be the instructional leader, facilities expert, budget analyst, emotional support human, political strategist, and PR rep... all while building a culture where people feel safe to grow.

> **Systems are important, but people matter more in leadership.**

They don't teach you that in school. But we're going to teach it here.

This book is for the leader who's ready to fully show up in their organization. The one who knows leadership is human work. The one who's not afraid to listen first, ask better questions, and start slow in order to lead boldly.

Stand firm. Lead with intention. The real work starts here.

Let's begin.

CHAPTER 1

The Plan No One Gave You

The Invisible Expectations of Leadership

From the second you accept the role, the expectations begin. Before you even set foot on campus, people have already formed ideas about you—based on what they've heard, what they've experienced in the past, or what they fear might happen next. Some want you to shake things up. Others hope you change nothing at all. You walk in carrying their hopes, their baggage, and especially their assumptions.

But here's the thing: nobody says this out loud.

Instead, you walk into a space already loaded with unspoken tension. You're expected to be decisive but approachable. Strong but not intimidating. A visionary but also practical. Somehow, you're supposed to know exactly what to do, even though you're still learning where the bathroom is!

What no one tells you is that most people are watching, not to see what you'll do, but to see if they can trust you.

And that trust? It's not earned by having all the answers; it's built in the moments when answers are unclear, but you show up anyway.

Why Most Entry Plans Fall Flat

A lot of leaders start with a polished 90-day plan. It looks great on paper... the scheduled meetings, data reviews, and the quick wins.

It's what conventional leadership wisdom recommends: gain momentum early, establish your credibility, deliver visible impact.

Michael Watkins, in *The First 90 Days*, popularized this idea in corporate and executive leadership spaces. And in many industries, it makes sense.

But in schools? It often falls flat.

And real life hits.

You inherit years of mistrust. Relationships that need healing. Staff who've weathered five principals in six years. Students carrying trauma, no walkthrough checklist will ever show you.

That's why this book offers something different... not a sprint toward early wins, but a deliberate invitation to start slow, so you can lead bold.

Leadership is presence.

It's how you respond when the room gets quiet, when the question catches you off guard, when the answer isn't obvious.

— 66 —

Leadership is presence.

—— 99 —

It's in how you listen when someone takes a risk and tells you the truth.

That's what builds trust.

The best leaders I know didn't start with a flashy rollout. They started by paying attention. They built trust before they made moves, and they learned the story before they tried to rewrite it.

The Myth of Proving vs. the Power of Listening

There's a huge pressure to prove yourself early. Fix something fast. Announce your vision. Make your mark. And sure... there's a time for that.

But in those first 90 days? Listening will take you further than any speech ever will.[1]

Listening builds trust. It slows your reaction time. It helps you see patterns instead of problems.

And let's be real—your team doesn't need another big promise. They need someone who sees them.

Leaders who start with listening tend to earn long-term credibility—not because they had the right answers, but because they asked the right questions. Listening doesn't mean sitting in silence and nodding. It means staying fully present. Asking follow-up questions. Paying attention to what's being said but more importantly... what's not being

---

[1] This aligns with Shane Safir's "90/10 Listening Campaign" from The Listening Leader, which encourages new leaders to listen 90% of the time and talk just 10% during their entry phase. My own approach was born from that same spirit—one rooted in lived experience, not theory alone.

said. Validating without rushing to fix. Following up on the hard stuff. Staying curious longer than you're comfortable.

When you listen well, people begin to let down their guard. And when people let down their guard, that's when the real work can begin.

If your staff has experienced frequent leadership turnover, they've likely developed emotional calluses. They've learned not to get too hopeful, not to say too much, and definitely not to trust too fast. Your job is not to break those walls down with charisma. It's to consistently show up in a way that lets those walls lower on their own.

You don't earn that with a clever vision statement. You earn it by learning people's names. By remembering what matters to them. By showing up when you said you would. And most of all... by listening to understand.

Researchers like Michael Fullan and Linda Darling-Hammond have been saying this for years—trust and connection are the bedrock of any real school transformation. And it's not just research, it's real life. Leaders who listen well, lead well.

Recent neuroscience backs it up. When people feel heard, their brains literally relax. They stop bracing for harm and start leaning into connection. That connection is where change begins.

Your Invitation to Lead Differently

You're not expected to have it all figured out. There's no need to walk in on day one with a polished vision statement, a color-coded plan, and a confident smile masking your inner panic. This is about leadership, not performance or pretense. You're not here to impress, you're here to lead.

You get to pause and breathe. You get to listen before speaking and observe without immediately reacting. You get to hold space for the complexity around you... without rushing to control it.

This is not a test of how quickly you can act. It's an invitation to design with care. Because what you choose to do—and not do—in those first 90 days will echo for years.

You are allowed to be a learner, listener, and a thoughtful observer. You are allowed to ask questions that others avoid. To sit with discomfort. To say, "I'm still learning."

That doesn't make you weak. That makes you wise. Strategic. And Human.

The truth is, the strongest leaders aren't the loudest in the room. They're the ones who know how to read it. And you? You're here because you want to lead differently. You're ready to reject performative leadership in favor of something deeper, more honest, and more transformative.

So if you've been waiting for a leadership plan that reflects real work—the messy, beautiful, complex work of guiding humans through change—this is it.

This is the unspoken plan. The one no one gave you—until now.

This is your invitation to lead differently.

Reflection Prompt

Before you move into the next chapter, take a moment to reflect:

- What expectations are you carrying into your new role—spoken or unspoken?

- Where do you feel pressure to perform instead of listen?

- What would it look like to give yourself permission to enter with curiosity instead of certainty?

This next chapter shifts the focus from strategy to soul. It's not about what you know—it's about how you show up. Chapter 2 is about connection, culture, and the human work that leadership demands.

Leadership Is Human Work

This work goes beyond knowing the standards; it requires knowing your people. Not knowing of them. Not knowing where they went to school or what their classroom theme is. I mean, really **knowing them.**

Knowing what lights them up. What weighs them down. What they're afraid to say out loud. What makes them feel seen and what makes them shut down. This kind of knowing doesn't happen by accident. It happens on purpose.

Leadership programs spend a lot of time on budgets, legal codes, instructional strategies, and organizational theory. And yes, you'll absolutely need every bit of that at some point. But it won't be what gets you through your hardest days.

What leadership prep programs don't tell you is that the real work lives in the space between people. It lives in body language during a hard conversation. It's in the hallway check-in that reveals what data never could. And it's also in the quiet moments when someone decides if they trust you... or not.

These are the moments that determine whether your plan will land, whether your staff will show up wholeheartedly, and whether your leadership will last. This is the work that builds a culture where people don't just comply—they care.

You can have the best plan in the world. But if people don't feel safe with you, they'll resist even the best ideas. **People don't follow strategy. They follow connection.**

And connection isn't built through performance. It's built through presence.

The Data No Spreadsheet Will Show You

Yes, data matters. But so does the look on your custodian's face when you greet them. So does the tone your secretary uses when she answers the phone. So does the question your newest teacher is afraid to ask in a staff meeting. So does the student who used to say good morning but now keeps their head down. So does the eye roll during your staff presentation, or the awkward silence after you ask for feedback. And so does the teacher who stops leaving their door open.

This kind of data? It's invisible. But it tells the truth.

Invisible data lives in the sighs between meetings. In who's missing from the table. In the way staff linger after a meeting... or how quickly they pack up and leave. It shows up in how often people volunteer ideas, in who speaks up when it's hard, and in who has stopped speaking altogether.

You won't find it in a spreadsheet, but it's the most honest data you'll ever get.

It's in the paraeducator who volunteers to run lunch duty every day but suddenly stops showing up. It's in the student who waits until everyone leaves before asking for help.

These are signals. Invitations. Quiet data waiting for leadership to notice.

Invisible data tells you when trust is being built—or eroded. When morale is rising—or quietly crumbling. It tells you if your vision is landing—or being politely ignored.

Most culture problems don't start with conflict. They start with absence. Absence of clarity, curiosity, time, and noticing. School culture breaks, not with a bang, but with a slow drift into disconnection.

That's why this work matters so much. Not because it's soft, but because it's the most strategic thing you can do as a leader: read the room before you run the play.

In *The Fifth Discipline*, Peter Senge reminds us that real learning gets to the heart of what it means to be human. And that's what leadership is... helping people learn, grow, and belong in systems that weren't always built for them.

Connection Over Control

The job will always pull you toward control: Budgets. Compliance. Timelines. Policies. Performance reviews.

But the role that transforms a campus happens through connection, not compliance.

Let's get real for a moment—do you like to be controlled? No one does. It strips away autonomy. It dulls creativity and builds quiet resentment. When people feel controlled, they start to protect themselves. They play small. They keep their heads down and their heart's guarded. And over time, even your best people will stop bringing their full selves to the work.

Control creates compliance. But connection builds commitment.

Real leadership is messy. Emotional. Layered. It's walking into a room full of people with different needs, triggers, and backstories... and trying to move them forward together.

Connection is when a teacher feels safe enough to say, "I'm struggling." It's when a classified staff member feels seen by leadership... not as a role, but as a human being. It's when your team stops asking, "Do I have to do this?" and starts asking, "How can I help?"

It's when a principal knows their custodian's birthday... and makes a big deal about it. It's when a school leader pauses the agenda to ask how someone's parent is doing... and means it. It's when a supervisor checks in after a tough IEP, or sits next to the teacher who's been crying during prep. It's not complicated, but it's incredibly rare.

Connection changes the tone in the staff lounge, the energy in the hallway, and the way your people respond when things get hard.

This isn't feel-good fluff... it's the real, foundational work that everything else depends on.

Culture doesn't respond to pressure. It responds to presence.

The best leaders I know don't command culture—they cultivate it.

How You Show Up > What You Know

Your energy introduces you before your words do. Your presence speaks louder than your policies. And your ability to make people feel seen, heard, and valued will carry you further than any textbook strategy ever could.

The title alone doesn't grant you trust. Trust is built in the way a leader shows up, day after day. You can't script school culture. That's shaped by a leader's steady, genuine presence.

People remember how you showed up in the hallway after a tough day. They remember whether you made time when they were hurting. They remember if you noticed or if you remembered something that is important to them.

Ultimately, leadership has less to do with knowing everything and more to do with earning the trust of others.

When the Humans Hit the Wall

Six years into my superintendency, I hit a wall—and so did my staff.

I remember feeling the shift like a slap. The energy was off. No one wanted to take on anything extra. Collaboration was lagging. People were clocking in, doing the minimum, and checking out. These were the same incredible educators who had powered through COVID, adapted overnight, and showed up for kids in ways most people will never understand. And now? They were done. And honestly... so was I.

We were all running on fumes. But instead of naming it, we were quietly pulling away from each other.

It was right before our annual staff retreat. And I remember thinking—I can't lead us into a new year if we're already starting broken. Something had to shift. So I did something simple: I asked.

I sent out an anonymous survey. No agenda. No leading questions. Just space for honesty.

Because I had worked so hard on building solid relationships from the beginning, I knew they would respond truthfully. I trusted that they'd tell me what I needed to hear... and they did.

But what helped me most was this: there was a theme.

I expected to hear about workload, or new initiatives, or stress from shifting expectations. But what came back, over and over, was this:

The relationships had slipped.

We weren't connected. Not to each other. Not to the work. Not even to ourselves.

School had become a machine. Fast, reactive, relentless. Our personal lives had filled every spare corner with stress and obligations. There was no margin. No joy. No time. And the thing we needed most—the thing that had always made our staff special—had quietly taken a back seat to the busyness.

What I realized next hit even harder: the system didn't just break down because of burnout. It broke down because the leader—me—was burnt out.

That kind of depletion doesn't just dim your energy. It reshapes your presence. When the leader isn't fully present, everyone can feel it.

That was my wake-up call.

It wasn't about programs. It wasn't about policies. It was about people. And when relationships suffer, the work does too.

That next layer? It's the story behind the signals. Every school has one. That's where we're headed next.

Reflection Prompt

Take a moment to reflect on your leadership presence:

- Where do you see invisible data showing up in your school or district?

- How are you currently building connections over compliance?

- When was the last time you paused to notice how someone was really doing?

- Write down one small shift you can make this week to show up with presence, not just position.

CHAPTER 3

Start With Story- Diagnose Before You Design

Every school has a story.

Sometimes it's told in murals on the wall and trophies in the case.

Sometimes it's whispered in the staff lounge, passed between grade levels, or etched into "the way things have always been."

You inherit that story the moment you walk through the door.

Some of it is beautiful with long-standing traditions, inside jokes, that one custodian everyone loves. Some of it is heavy, centered around deep distrust, wounds from previous leadership, systems built for survival instead of success.

Here's the hard truth:

Skipping the story means risking the solution—without context, even your best efforts can miss the mark.

Too many leaders rush to action—not out of carelessness, but from a sincere desire to help. But when you move too quickly, you risk mistaking symptoms for root causes. You fix surface-level issues while the real ones remain untouched. You implement changes that don't stick because they weren't grounded in the truth of the place.

If you want lasting change, you have to honor where people have been before you lead them somewhere new.

You have to slow down long enough to ask:

What do people really believe about this organization?

Where did those beliefs come from?

Who holds influence here... and why?

What systems are quietly shaping what's possible?

The story is complex and often hidden. It's layered and unfinished. At times—painful.

But it's always there... waiting to be heard.

When I first arrived in my district, I sat down with every stakeholder I could: staff members, parents, board members, students, and community members... and just listened. I wasn't there to impress them. I was there to understand.

The stories they shared weren't easy. Families who never felt heard, while others were favored. Long board meetings that had turned into unruly shouting matches month after month. Teachers who had been targeted if they talked about what they were experiencing.

The board was absolutely exhausted. The staff was discouraged after years of not being heard, and because of this, staff turnover was high. Students felt the tension but didn't always have the words for it. Some parents were frustrated and fearful, unsure if they could trust leadership again, while others couldn't understand how their beloved Superintendent/Principal had ended up in the hot seat. Community members were confused, divided, and deeply concerned about the future of the school they had always supported. Everyone was still carrying the emotional weight of years of dysfunction and distrust.

As I listened to story after story, one thing became clear: this wasn't a place where a quick fix would work. This wasn't a time for sweeping declarations or bold changes. What this school needed was healing, trust-building, and clarity. And also, a leader who would take the time to truly understand the layers beneath the surface.

In that moment, I knew my first job wasn't to change things... it was to really learn the story. Because until I understood where we had been, I couldn't lead us to what could be.

Observe, Ask, Listen, Repeat

Learning your school's story develops over time through intentional choices and a practice of staying curious. You learn the story by showing up consistently and noticing the things most people overlook. It happens in small moments. In the hallway conversations between classes. In the way staff members interact at dismissal, and the looks exchanged in a meeting when something sensitive comes up. These moments are filled with clues and they're really easy to miss if you're rushing to check boxes.

Start by simply paying attention—to everything. Listen as the administrative assistant greets people when they walk through the door.

Sit in classrooms and watch the interactions amongst the students and staff. Grab lunch in the staff lounge. Sit amongst the community at student games. Notice how students line up, how adults guide transitions, and what the small moments reveal. Just observe... no fixing, no judging. These aren't just logistics but rather culture in motion.

Ask questions that open doors:

"What's something people here are really proud of?"

"What do you wish others understood about your work?"

"What's one thing you'd never want to lose?"

"If you could change anything, what would you start with?"

And then—listen. Not to respond. Not to strategize. Just to understand.

When people feel genuinely heard, they give you something invaluable: the truth.

Some of the most powerful insights I've ever gained came not from a formal meeting, but from walking a lap around campus with a staff member who needed to vent. Or from watching who sat with whom at lunch. Or from a side comment a student made after receiving a referral that revealed so much more.

Like the day I noticed upper-grade students in our after-school program were suddenly racking up behavior referrals. These were kids who rarely got in trouble. Something wasn't adding up. So I asked.

Turns out, they were going from 45 minutes of PE during the day straight into another 45 minutes of structured physical activity after school. They were tired. They just wanted a break.

I gave them a voice and choice to redesign that time. Same requirements—but now, it was on their terms. Referrals dropped to zero. All because one comment sparked a conversation... and someone listened.

You won't learn everything in one conversation, and you won't always hear what you want to hear. But if you show up consistently, humbly, and with genuine curiosity—people will talk. And when they do, they're handing you a map.

A map of what matters. A map of where the cracks are. A map of what's sacred, and what's broken.

That map is what helps you lead with both clarity and compassion.

Once you've mapped the story, the next step is to examine the system that's been quietly reinforcing it.

Systems Are Designed to Produce Exactly What They're Producing

It's easy to look at surface-level problems and think they're about people: a disengaged staff, poor student behavior, and low parent involvement. But these aren't individual failures—they're system signals.

Every school is perfectly structured to produce the results it's getting.[2] If something isn't working, it's not about who... It's about what and how.

Systems are like currents. They quietly pull people along, reinforcing habits, expectations, and norms, whether or not those norms are healthy. If you want to change outcomes, you have to find the current.

You have to name it, trace it, and ask what it's protecting.

Is your discipline data skewed toward one group of students? That's not just a behavior problem—it's a system design issue.

Is your staff morale low? That's not just a mindset issue—it's often about broken feedback loops, unclear priorities, or inconsistent leadership.

Is your instructional practice fragmented? That's not about a lack of effort—it's often about a lack of common language, planning time, or shared vision.

The point isn't to blame the system. The point is to see it clearly and start shifting it with intention.

Until you understand what the system is designed to do, you'll waste energy trying to change what it's perfectly built to protect.

---

[2]Paraphrased from Dr. W. Edwards Deming's discussion of systems, variation, and continuous improvement.

Start by noticing...

Who speaks up during meetings—and who never does.

What happens after someone makes a mistake—are they supported or blamed?

Which students are praised publicly—and which are quietly overlooked?

These small signals tell you more about a system's design than any manual ever could.

Remember: The purpose of systems thinking is to examine the patterns behind harmful behavior rather than excuse it. When we shift our focus from blame to design, we stop reacting and start rebuilding. That's where sustainable change begins.

Red Flags & Root Causes

As you prepare to step into your new role, you'll need to be ready to listen, observe, and see your system with eyes wide open. You might not know exactly what to look for at first, but you'll begin to notice signals—patterns, behaviors, or tensions that feel off. These aren't random. They're the system trying to tell you something. Most of what you'll see first are just symptoms. The deeper work is figuring out what's underneath.

The staff that's resistant to change? They are likely exhausted from years of turnover and broken promises.

The team that always needs direction? They may have been conditioned to believe that decisions are always top-down.

The inconsistent classroom expectations? That's likely not a teacher problem. It's a systems issue around training, clarity, and collaboration.

Here's the key: don't stop at what's visible. Ask,

"What's underneath this?"

What history shaped this behavior?

What beliefs are being protected here?

What patterns have we normalized... and at what cost?

Root causes often live in the unspoken:

A toxic norm that's never been named.

A leader's legacy that still lingers.

A fear that's become part of the culture.

Your job is to diagnose patterns, not people. That's how you shift the system without creating more harm.

Identifying the true root cause doesn't just solve the issue. It liberates the people affected by it.

Reflection Prompt

Before you move into the next chapter, take a few minutes to reflect:

- What red flags have you witnessed in schools or districts you've been part of?

- Which behaviors or patterns might actually be signals of something deeper?

- What systems or habits might be reinforcing the outcomes you're walking into?

- Write down your insights. The more clearly you can name what you're stepping into, the more intentionally you can lead through it.

CHAPTER 4

Build Trust Like a Leader, Not a Manager

Trust doesn't come from position. It's built in the moments that don't make the agenda but define your leadership. So when you step into your new role, walking the campus, asking questions, and noticing the patterns, know this: none of it will matter if people don't trust you. That's the difference between a manager and a leader. Managers focus on tasks. Leaders build trust. In schools, trust isn't optional—it's oxygen.

It often begins before you even realize it. It starts the moment you pause in the hallway to greet a custodian by name. The way you listen in a staff meeting without rushing to solve. The choice to follow up after someone shares a worry. These aren't grand gestures; they're early signals. They tell people whether you're here to manage them or lead with them.

Trust is built in the quiet follow-up. The extra minute you stay after a staff meeting to check in on someone's face. The email you return when it would've been easier to ignore. The honesty you offer when the answer is "I don't know... yet."

Brené Brown reminds us in *Dare to Lead* (2018), "trust is earned in small moments." It's the tiny, often overlooked choices that end up building the strongest foundations, and it begins when people realize they're seen not just for their role, but for who they are.

The Trust Curve

Not everyone starts from the same point on the trust curve. Some people want to believe in you. They're hopeful. Curious. Others are skeptical. They've seen leaders come and go. They're waiting for you to slip. And some? They're done. They've been let down too many times. Your job isn't to win them over all at once; it's to show up in ways that slowly shift the curve. One interaction at a time.

Micro-Moments That Matter Most

The trust you're building won't come from a single meeting or a perfectly written email. It comes from how you show up when no one's keeping score.

When you hold the door open for a student carrying a project. When you catch a teacher's eye after a tough lesson and simply nod in solidarity. When you remember someone's dog is sick, or that their child had a game last night.

These moments seem small. But in a school setting where people are constantly assessing whether leadership is safe, human, and present—micro-moments matter most.

These are the moments that say: I see you. I care. You matter more than the to-do list.

You don't have to be perfect. You have to be present.

The Trust Ledger

> You don't have to be perfect. You have to be present.

Every interaction either deposits into or withdraws from the emotional bank account you have with your team. You may not always see the balance, but your team feels it. And in the beginning, you're starting from scratch—or, in some cases, from a deficit left by the leaders before you.

You're inheriting emotional history, not just an organization chart. The question isn't just: Do people trust you? It's: Do people trust leadership?

That's a different question and one you have to answer with your actions.

You build trust when you keep your word. You build trust when you name the hard things. You build trust when you show people they matter more than your agenda.

Trust doesn't come quickly... but when it does, it changes everything. Once it's earned, you won't need to persuade people to follow. They'll choose to.

A Moment That Built the Ledger

It's 8:10. Class starts in five minutes. My phone rings. It's one of our teachers, and she's in tears.

Her dream home, the one she designed from the ground up, the one she was just weeks away from moving into... had flooded. This wasn't just a house. It was her American dream. As the daughter of immigrants, this moment represented everything she and her family had worked for. And now, water was pouring into the very foundation of that dream.

She called, crying, because she needed to leave. She knew she couldn't emotionally invest in her students that day, not after everything that had just happened.

This wasn't a decision I had to think twice about. When someone is hurting, people come first... always. And that belief guides every move I make as a leader.

Even though I didn't have a sub. Even though class was starting in minutes. Even though I could already feel the ripple effect of her absence through the building, I told her to go. We would figure it out.

Because in that moment, what mattered most wasn't logistics. It was her.

That decision didn't just help her; it told every staff member who heard the story that I saw them. That I wasn't going to lead from policy alone. That trust goes both ways.

And that's what this next section is about: how those moments—quiet, unmeasured, inconvenient... become the currency of trust.

Reflection Prompt

- Think back to your last week—in leadership, in life, in relationships with others. Where did micro-moments happen?

- Who lingered after a meeting? Who looked like they needed to be asked, "Are you okay?" Where did you follow through—or forget to?

- List two small actions you could take this week that might shift the trust curve. Then do them—not for recognition, but because trust is built in the moments no one's measuring.

CHAPTER 5

Make Meaning from the Mess-Find the Patterns That Matter

Whether you're days away from starting or already knee-deep in your new role, one thing is certain: the smartest leaders don't walk in with answers—they walk in with questions. You're not just here to manage a to-do list. You're here to read the room, decode the culture, and figure out what's really going on beneath the surface.

This is where real leadership begins—not in the spotlight, but in the stillness. Not with the loudest voice, but with the most observant mind.

You're either starting to see—or preparing to see—the invisible threads that hold your system together: the side glances during meetings, the teacher who used to share ideas and now stays silent, and the hallway conversations that carry more weight than any formal agenda. These are more than moments: they're messages. And they're waiting for you to pay attention.

Whether you're imagining what's ahead or already feeling the weight of what you've stepped into, the next step is the same: ***make meaning before you make moves.***

Listening is powerful. It builds trust and opens doors. But leadership requires more than hearing. It requires meaning-making.

> Listening is powerful. It builds trust and opens doors.

It's one thing to gather stories; It's another to trace patterns. It's one thing to spot problems; It's another to see the system behind them.

This chapter is where the diagnosis gets deeper. You're no longer just walking the halls and building trust—you're beginning to connect the dots.

In every school, there are patterns hiding in plain sight. These are the patterns that quietly shape what's possible. They live in who speaks up in meetings, who doesn't. In how conflict is handled—or avoided. In what's rewarded, and what's ignored. These patterns are the pulse of your culture. And if you want real change, you need to learn how to read them.

This is where many leaders go wrong. They either:

Dismiss the mess as personality problems, or

Rush to fix the symptoms without understanding the roots.

But the best leaders do something different. They pause. They sift. They get curious. They ask: *What is this mess trying to tell me?*

This is how you begin to move from listening to learning. From learning to clarity. From clarity to strategy.

Strategy without story is hollow. And story without systems thinking is incomplete.

The work of making meaning is both analytical and human. It's sitting with discomfort long enough to see what it reveals. It's resisting the urge to act until you understand the why.

It's what separates performative leaders from transformative ones.

Let's begin the work of finding the patterns that matter most.

Pattern Spotting in Real Life

You won't find these patterns on a spreadsheet. You'll find them in the way people react when a certain topic comes up. In who rolls their eyes when a new initiative is announced. In the way staff meetings go silent when a particular voice starts speaking, or how quickly they end when certain perspectives aren't in the room at all.

These aren't isolated incidents. They're signals. And great leaders learn to follow them like breadcrumbs.

Start noticing:

- Who always gets praised—and who consistently gets overlooked?
- Who volunteers their ideas freely—and who checks out quietly?
- Which classrooms buzz with energy—and which feel heavy or disconnected?
- Where do students linger—and where do they avoid?

- Who gets looped in early—and who hears things last?
- What procedures cause stress every time they're implemented—and no one questions them anymore?

These are not just one-off frustrations. They're clues pointing to deeper systemic norms, power dynamics, and unspoken rules.

When you see a pattern that feels off, don't rush to fix it. Sit with it. Ask questions. Work to reveal the story under the surface.

Often, what we interpret as pushback is actually someone protecting themselves. What we label as disinterest may just be confusion no one felt safe enough to name. And what we call disengagement is often exhaustion that builds up after years of trying, adapting, and not being heard.

When it feels like a people issue, it's usually a signal that the system has been quietly failing them.

You're not here to fix people.

You're here to understand the conditions they've been navigating, often invisibly, for far too long.

That's how you lead with compassion.

That's how you make change that actually lasts.

Make the Implicit Explicit

Once you've spotted the patterns, your next move is simple but bold: name them.

Most school cultures are built on unspoken truths. Everyone knows who has quiet power, which topics are avoided, which traditions are sacred, and what unwritten rules govern behavior. But very few people are willing to say these things out loud—especially those in leadership.

But here's the truth: you can't change what you won't name.

Naming things—gently, honestly, and without blame—is what creates the space for something healthier to grow in its place.

This doesn't mean calling people out or turning every meeting into a group therapy session. It means learning how to name what's underneath without triggering more defensiveness. It's saying things like:

"I've noticed we have a lot of side conversations after meetings. What's not being said out loud?"

"I see that new ideas often stall out... Is there a fear of failure at play here?"

"We keep saying we value collaboration, but we're not building in time or systems for it. What's getting in the way?"

"It feels like there's some hesitation around this change. What's the real story behind the resistance?"

You can also name the positive patterns:

"I've noticed that students feel really safe in your classroom... What are you doing that others could learn from?"

"That staff meeting had energy and participation we haven't seen in a while. Let's unpack what made that possible."

Naming both the fractures and the bright spots helps build a culture where truth isn't scary—it's strategic. And it sends a clear message:

You're not here to sweep things under the rug. You're here to build trust by telling the truth and inviting others to do the same.

From Patterns to Priorities

Once you've named the patterns, your next step is turning insight into action—

and that means deciding what deserves your attention first.

Not every pattern you notice needs an action plan. Some things just need to be acknowledged. Others need to be watched. But a few? A few patterns are so foundational, so closely tied to student outcomes or staff well-being, that they can't wait. Those are the ones you move on.

This is where many new leaders get stuck. Not because they don't see what's wrong, but because they try to fix too much at once.

So how do you decide where to focus?

Ask yourself:

What's causing the most day-to-day friction—not just for me, but for the people I serve?

What's been brought up more than once—in different ways, by different people?

Which issues are quietly affecting multiple areas of the school?

What's being tolerated—but shouldn't be?

What's happening frequently enough—or painfully enough—that it's shaping the culture?

Then ask the most important question of all:

What's worth designing for right now — and what can wait?

Maybe the loudest issue isn't the most urgent one. Maybe the thing that's never brought up in meetings—but always shows up in hallway whispers—is where the real work needs to begin.

You don't need to have a solution for everything. You need to choose what matters most and give it your best energy.

That's how you move from awareness to action. Not by fixing everything. But by fixing what matters most—first.

Reflection Prompt

Take a moment to reflect:

- What patterns have you noticed—or anticipate noticing— that quietly shape the culture?

- Which unspoken rules or beliefs need to be named so they can be addressed?

- Of all the patterns you've seen so far, which feels most urgent to understand more deeply?

- Write them down. Then circle the one you feel most pulled to act on—not because it's loud, but because it's real.

This is your starting point.

CHAPTER 6

Rebuild What You Didn't Break- Lead Through the Trust Gap

Earlier, we explored how trust is built in the micro-moments of everyday leadership. But what happens when trust wasn't just absent but was broken before you arrived?

Not every leader gets to start fresh.

Sometimes, you walk into a school where trust was fractured long before your arrival. Decisions were made behind closed doors. Staff felt ignored or blamed. Families gave up on being heard. And now, you wear the title and carry the weight of leadership that hurt more than it helped.

You didn't create the wounds. But they show up in your inbox, your staff meetings, and your hallway conversations. This chapter is about what to do when trust is missing, and you're the one expected to restore it.

You can't build a future on a foundation of fear.

You have to repair it—one choice, one conversation, one act of integrity at a time.

Rebuilding Trust in Real Time

Trust won't be rebuilt in a single moment or even in your first 90 days. But it can start immediately.

Not with a big speech and not with a strategic plan.

It will get rebuilt with presence, proof, and predictable, human leadership.

You're not just rebuilding trust with individuals; you're reshaping belief in the role itself. That requires you to:

Follow through on the small stuff. If you say you'll check on something? Do it. Can't answer a question? Circle back. Trust is built when your word becomes reliable.

Say what you mean—and then back it up. Your words will lay the foundation, but your actions build the trust. When those two match, people start to believe.

Name what came before you. Unpacking all the history is not necessary. But you absolutely need to acknowledge it. A simple line like, "I know this school has seen a lot of change," invites healing without assigning blame.

Be visibly transparent. Share your process. Say things like, "Here's what I'm thinking, and here's what I'm still unsure of." People trust what they understand.

Build feedback rituals. Create anonymous surveys, 1:1 check-ins, or listening circles. Trust deepens when people feel safe to speak...and confident they'll be heard.

Create clear communication systems. Confusion erodes trust, but clarity strengthens it. Let people know when, how, and why updates are coming — and how to voice concerns without fear.

Be consistent. Culture always remembers. If you protect someone in public but undermine them in private, people notice. Lead, like every move, teaches people what to expect from you.

Lead like a human. Check in after a hard IEP. Ask about someone's family. Show up in crisis and in calm. When people feel seen beyond their job, trust becomes possible.

When trust has been broken, your title alone won't fix it. But your patterns, your presence, and your follow-through? That's how you begin to rebuild what was lost.

When You Didn't Break the Trust — But You Carry the Title

This might be one of the hardest things about stepping into leadership: you are not starting from zero.

You're stepping into someone else's story—a story that may include betrayal, disconnection, or years of silence. You didn't cause the harm, but you now wear the badge that represents it.

The gut-punch: it doesn't matter if you're different. Not at first. Because people aren't reacting to *you*, they're reacting to what your title has come to represent.

They're not testing your credibility.

They're protecting themselves from being disappointed again.

So when someone is short with you in a meeting...

When they avoid eye contact...

When they copy five people on an email that could've gone to you directly...

It's not always about you—but it is yours to carry now.

This is the part no one talks about in leadership prep:

That, at its core, the biggest barrier you'll face may not be a policy or a budget but the invisible grief your community is still carrying... and the only way to lead through that is to choose presence over performance.

To say:

"I wasn't here when that happened, but I understand it hurt."

"You don't have to trust me yet—let me earn that."

"You've been through a lot. I don't take that lightly."

There's no need to apologize for decisions made before your time. But recognizing their impact is essential. That's the line between defensiveness and true leadership.

No, you can't undo the past. But you can be the one who doesn't pretend it never happened. The one who stays present, even when it's uncomfortable, and the one who listens without needing to explain it away. Who says, "I see you"—and means it, with actions that follow through.

That's what begins to shift things. Not perfection. Not performance... but presence.

Build a Culture That Outlasts You

If trust depends on *you* always being present, it's not a system—it's a personality.

And when that personality leaves, the trust often leaves with it.

Great leaders don't just build trust through relationships. They embed trust into the way the school operates so that belief, belonging, and transparency become cultural norms, not individual habits.

Here's what that looks like:

Document what's been unsaid. Most schools have a hidden curriculum of norms and assumptions. Make them visible. Write down the "unwritten rules" and turn them into real agreements the team can examine, shift, or discard.

Normalize psychological safety. This isn't just about being nice—it's about creating conditions where people feel safe to take risks, offer feedback, and challenge ideas. If people are afraid to speak the truth, you're building trust on quicksand.

Create trust-building routines. Rituals matter. Build in predictable touchpoints: weekly check-ins, gratitude circles, post-observation reflections. The goal isn't structure for structure's sake—it's consistency that sends the message: You matter here.

Decentralize leadership. Share decision-making. Invite staff into the process early, not just to give input, but to help shape what comes next. The more people see themselves in the school's direction, the more they'll protect it.

Honor integrity—not just outcomes. When someone holds a boundary, tells the truth, or owns a mistake, don't gloss over it. That's how trust is built. Those are the moments that model the culture you're trying to build.

The goal isn't just to be a trusted leader. It's to leave behind a school where trust is simply *how things are done around here.*

Someday, you won't be in this role anymore.

And when that happens, the true test of your leadership will be this:

Did the culture hold?

The goal isn't just to be a trusted leader. It's to leave behind a school where trust is simply how things are done around here.

Reflection Prompt

Before moving forward, take a moment to reflect:

- Where do you see trust thriving—and where is it quietly eroding?

- How have past leadership patterns shaped current staff behaviors?

- What's one way you can begin earning trust this week—not with a big gesture, but with quiet consistency?

Write it down. Small, repeated actions—not grand declarations—are what rebuild belief. Once trust begins to rebuild, the real learning can begin—not just for students, but for adults too.

CHAPTER 7

Shape the Learning Culture

You're not the top evaluator.

You're not the expert in every subject.

And you're not expected to have all the answers.

But you are the one who sets the tone for what learning feels like, not just for students, but for every adult in the building.

Your job isn't to micromanage instruction. It's to create a culture where growth is safe, expected, and real. Where reflection is part of the daily rhythm. Where instructional conversations aren't scary. And where feedback isn't a formality, it's just how we work.

Whether you're walking into a well-oiled system or total chaos, remember this:

Your presence will matter more than any plan.

Staff won't rise to your résumé. They'll rise—or retreat—to the level of culture you build.

If you want students to thrive, you have to begin by shaping the learning that happens behind every classroom door.

Let's start there.

Set the Vision Before You Set the Expectation

Before you can coach, support, or grow instructional practice, your team needs to understand what learning looks like under your leadership. That doesn't mean rolling out a binder or dropping a PowerPoint deck on day one. It means communicating your learning values clearly and modeling them consistently.

Ask yourself:

What does high-quality teaching look, sound, and feel like?

What beliefs about learning do I want my team to share?

What does it mean to grow professionally in this space?

Your vision doesn't have to be perfect, but it does have to be clear.

The clearest vision is the one you embody.

If you want teachers to be reflective, model reflection out loud. If you want collaboration, invite co-creation. If you want vulnerability, start with your own.

This is how instructional vision takes root—not through mandates, but through modeling.

When people feel your why, it stops being *your* work. It starts becoming theirs, too.

That's where we go next: what adult learning actually looks like when it's done well.

What Adult Learning Looks Like in Practice

Adult learning isn't about sit-and-get. It's not about clock hours, sign-in sheets, or PD that's forgotten before the week is over. Real adult learning is reflective, embedded, and alive in the daily work.

It looks like:

Teachers asking for feedback, not because they have to, but because they trust it will help them grow.

PLC meetings that feel like real collaboration—not compliance checks.

Staff meetings that make people think, not just sit.

Leaders modeling curiosity, not perfection.

It also looks like:

Having protocols in place so tough conversations feel productive, not personal.

Using walkthroughs not to "catch" teachers, but to understand the experience of learners.

Making space for adults to reflect—not just on what's being taught, but how it's landing.

Here's the thing: adult learning doesn't always need to come from you. In fact, the most sustainable cultures are the ones where:

Teachers learn from each other.

Classified staff are included in professional learning.

Ideas bubble up, not just trickle down.

As the lead learner, your role is to create the conditions:

Where learning is visible.

Where growth is celebrated.

Where reflection is routine.

Because when adults are growing, students are too.

Here's what that can look like in everyday practice:

Opening staff meetings with a shared learning question. Something simple like, "What's one instructional risk you've taken this month?" creates space for vulnerability and growth.

Designating a teacher-led segment in every meeting. Give space for peers to share a lesson, a tech tool, or a challenge they're navigating. This signals that everyone is a contributor to the learning culture.

Starting classroom walkthroughs with a wondering, not a checklist. Instead of "Did I see what was expected?" try "What are students doing, saying, and producing—and what does that tell us?"

Celebrating learning moves, not just achievement outcomes. Highlight a teacher who tried a new strategy. Applaud a paraeducator who facilitated an incredible student breakthrough. Recognize a staff member who brought a new idea to the table.

Building adult learning into the rhythm of the week. Instead of scheduling one-off PD days, carve out 10–15

minutes of learning every Wednesday or embed micro-reflection protocols into PLCs.

Coaching conversations that ask more than they tell.
Lead with: "What felt strong in that lesson?" or "What might you try
next time?" Empower people to reflect first, instead of defaulting to di-
rective feedback.

This isn't about adding more to people's plates—it's about shifting how we see the plate itself. Every moment in a school can either
reinforce a culture of compliance—or create a culture of growth.

You get to model that shift.

You get to lead that learning.

If you're a superintendent or district-level leader, your proximity to classrooms might feel more limited, but your impact on adult
learning is just as powerful. Your role is to create coherence, alignment,
and inspiration across multiple campuses. That starts by treating site
leaders as your lead learners.

It looks like:

**Modeling inquiry and reflection with your principals
and directors.** When you reflect openly on what you're learning and
how you're growing, you normalize learning at every level.

**Building instructional rounds into your leadership
team meetings.** Let principals and coaches visit each other's schools
with a lens for learning, not evaluation.

Asking questions like, "What learning is alive at your site?" or
"What conversations are happening in your PLCs?" These prompts com-
municate that you care about learning—not just logistics.

Celebrating growth stories at every board meeting. Highlight teacher-led innovations. Showcase how a site turned a challenge into a learning opportunity. Put adult learning front and center, even when the spotlight usually falls on student data.

Providing differentiated professional learning for leaders. One-size-fits-all PD doesn't grow strong site leaders. Support their unique growth needs, just like you would for teachers.

The best leaders know: culture flows from the top. If you model learning at the highest level, it gives permission for every leader, teacher, and staff member to do the same.

Learning isn't just for classrooms. It's the heartbeat of the entire system.

Let's move into how your presence—as a coach, not just a supervisor—makes that learning culture sustainable.

Observation vs. Evaluation: Shifting the Purpose of Presence

One of the most powerful signals you send as a leader is how—and why—you show up in classrooms.

If staff only see you with a clipboard in hand, scribbling notes in the back of the room, they'll brace for judgment. But when your presence feels like partnership, not performance management, everything changes.

Great leaders shift from evaluator to observer—not to lower expectations, but to build trust, understanding, and collective growth.

Here's the difference:

Evaluation says: "I'm here to rate you."

Observation says: "I'm here to learn alongside you."

Observation for learning looks like:

Dropping into classrooms regularly and informally.

Asking questions like, "What are you trying out today?" or "What are you hoping students walk away with?"

Following up with curiosity, not critique.

Noticing what students are doing, not just what the teacher is saying.

When educators feel seen and supported instead of watched and judged, they become more open to feedback, more willing to try something new, and more invested in the learning culture you're building.

Presence isn't about catching mistakes. It's about catching moments and using them to fuel growth.

For site leaders, this means being a frequent, calm, and curious presence in classrooms. Not just when observations are due—but often enough that teachers no longer tense up when you walk in.

It looks like:

Saying, "I'm here to learn, not to evaluate," and meaning it.

Taking notes about student engagement and asking reflective follow-ups like, "What do you think made that moment land so well?"

Leave a sticky note with a genuine question or a shout-out.

Building trust first, then layering in feedback over time.

These small shifts reposition the principal's role from compliance monitor to collaborative learner.

For district leaders, presence looks different, but it's just as important. Your "observation" might be sitting in on a PLC. Walking a school with a principal. Visiting a classroom side-by-side with a coach. Your questions matter more than your clipboard.

— 66 —

These small shifts reposition the principal's role from compliance monitor to collaborative learner.

— 99 —

Try:

"What are you seeing across classrooms that excites you?"

"How are your teachers experiencing the support we've provided?"

"Where do you feel your team is growing—and where are they stuck?"

District presence shouldn't be about micromanaging instruction. It should be about listening for system-wide signals, lifting up promising practices, and being a thinking partner for your site leaders.

The tone you set in these moments shapes how they show up in theirs.

Coaching Conversations That Build Capacity

Being present is just the start. The real growth comes through the conversations that follow.

Coaching isn't about fixing but rather expanding capacity. It's how we help people see what's possible, reflect more deeply, and take ownership of their practice.

Here's the key: coaching doesn't require a formal title. It requires intention.

Whether you're a site leader or a superintendent, your questions matter more than your answers. The best coaching conversations start with:

"What felt strong about that lesson?"

"What surprised you today?"

"What might you try next time?"

"What support would help you take the next step?"

From the site level:

Make time for informal check-ins that aren't tied to evaluation.

Use walkthrough data as a conversation starter, not a scoreboard.

Offer specific praise that connects to professional goals: "I noticed how you used student responses to shift your pacing—that kind of flexibility is powerful."

From the district level:

Create space in principal meetings for peer coaching—not just updates.

Use data as a doorway into reflection: "What's this telling us? What's missing?"

Resist the urge to lead with solutions. Instead, lead with curiosity.

Great coaching honors expertise while stretching practice.

It's not about delivering the answers. It's about helping people discover the ones they already hold.

This is how you build a culture of learners—not just employees.

Feedback That Fuels, Not Flattens

Feedback is one of the most powerful tools in a leader's toolkit—and one of the most misused.

When done poorly, feedback flattens. It shuts people down. It makes them feel judged, not supported. And over time, it chips away at trust.

But when feedback is rooted in curiosity, clarity, and care? It fuels growth. It becomes something people seek out, not brace themselves for.

Here's what fueling feedback looks like:

It starts with purpose. Why am I giving this feedback? Is it about growth, clarity, or ego? Be honest with yourself.

It centers the learner. Ask first: "What felt strong?" "What are you wondering about?" "Where do you want feedback?"

It focuses on practice, not personality. "When you used that prompt, student responses deepened" is very different from "You're a natural." One builds skills, the other flatters.

It's actionable. Vague praise and general critiques don't help anyone. Be specific. Be kind. Be direct.

From the site level:

Give feedback in proximity. Don't wait three weeks to talk about a lesson. Share quick insights the same day.

Build feedback into everyday routines—hallway chats, walk-throughs, or reflective emails.

Name the why: "I'm sharing this because I see your potential, and I want to help you grow."

From the district level:

Model healthy feedback in leadership team meetings. Celebrate strong thinking. Challenge ideas respectfully.

Ask for feedback yourself: "What's one way I could support you better?"

Create feedback loops that go both ways—between cabinet and principals, between departments and sites.

The goal isn't perfect feedback. It's a feedback culture. One where growth isn't a surprise, it's a shared commitment.

When feedback fuels instead of flattens, your team won't just improve—they'll thrive.

Reflection Prompt

Take a few moments to reflect:

- How are you currently modeling what it means to be a learner?

- Where in your week do you create space for adult learning—and where could you?

- When was the last time feedback felt energizing instead of evaluative?

- What's one small shift you could make this week to lead learning more intentionally?

Write down your reflections. Learning leadership starts with awareness and grows through action.

CHAPTER 8

When the Work Gets Hard-And People Push Back

Change sounds visionary—until it feels personal. And for many people, your leadership will feel personal. Not because of who you are, but because of what you represent:

A new direction, a shift in power, a disruption to the familiar—even if the familiar wasn't working.

This is when the work stops being theoretical.

This is when it gets real.

Not everyone will welcome your ideas. Not everyone will be ready.

Some days, the resistance will come from places you didn't expect: The teacher you trusted. The board member who backed you. The staff member who said, "I've got your back"—until you made a hard call.

In those moments, you'll be tempted to second-guess everything:

Am I leading wrong?

Did I move too fast?

Maybe I should've just kept the peace.

But here's what you need to know:

Pushback doesn't always mean you're failing. Sometimes it means you're doing something that finally matters.

When you ask people to think differently, work differently, or show up differently, it stirs things. That stirring is uncomfortable. But discomfort is part of growth.

Your job isn't to avoid resistance. It's to understand it and stay grounded when the ground feels shaky. To lead anyway.

Let's talk about how.

What Resistance Reveals—and What to Do With It

When the pushback comes, your first instinct might be to fix it or defend yourself against it. But what if you treated resistance not as a roadblock, but as a roadmap?

Every moment of resistance is pointing you to something deeper:

A belief that's being challenged.

A fear that's being activated.

A norm that's being disrupted.

A power dynamic that's being reshaped.

This is where many leaders get stuck. They either:

Over-explain to convince people they're right, or

Shut it down to avoid losing control.

Transformational leaders take a different approach. They lean in with curiosity.

They ask:

What is this resistance protecting?

What story is this person telling themselves, and how can I help reshape it?

What relationship do I need to strengthen in order to move forward?

Here's what to do *in the moment:*

Pause your reaction. When resistance hits, your nervous system will want to react—defend, explain, retreat. Don't. Breathe. Buy yourself a moment to think before speaking.

Name the emotion, not just the behavior. "I can see this is frustrating," goes further than "You're not being helpful." Honor the emotion—it softens the edge.

Don't chase compliance. You can force agreement, but you can't fake commitment. Aim for connection over control.

Zoom out. Ask yourself: Is this resistance a pattern or a one-off? Is it coming from one person or a system-wide signal? Resist the urge to personalize what might actually be institutional.

Respond with consistency. The best answer to resistance is steady leadership. Say what you mean. Do what you said. And keep showing up.

When you learn to read resistance like data—not drama—you lead with more clarity, not just control.

Lead Yourself First

Before you can lead others through resistance, you've got to walk yourself through it.

This is the part no one prepares you for. Resistance doesn't just test your leadership. It messes with your head. It slows your pace, shakes your confidence, and wears down your peace. You start questioning your timing. Wondering if you read the room wrong. And sometimes, yes—it feels personal. Like the people you thought had your back just disappeared.

That's real. But it doesn't have to take you out.

This is where leading from the inside matters most.

Stay grounded in your values. When pushback comes, your values are your compass. Go back to what you believe. Remember why you're here and who you're fighting for. Let that guide your next step—not fear, frustration, or ego.

Reflect, don't retreat. Not all pushback is rejection. Most of the time, it's feedback in disguise. Ask yourself: What's this trying to teach me? What's mine to own? What's not?

Get support. You need people in your corner—the ones who remind you why you started, especially when the weight of the job feels extremely heavy, or the noises are too loud. Find your people. Protect those relationships. Let them call you back to what matters when the noise tries to drown it out.

Lead without losing yourself. You can't lead well when you're overwhelmed or running on fumes. Step away.

Breathe. Move your body. Do what you need to come back centered and clear.

Trust the process. Resistance is a normal, even necessary, part of change. It doesn't mean you're failing. It means you're leading.

When you lead yourself through the hard parts with steadiness, your team doesn't just notice—they remember.

That's what builds credibility. That's what earns trust.

Not perfection. Presence.

Reflection Prompt: Leading Through the Pushback

Take a moment to reflect on your leadership through resistance:

- When pushback shows up, how do you tend to respond—emotionally, mentally, and behaviorally?

- What part of resistance triggers you the most—being misunderstood, challenged, or ignored?

> **"**
> Because resistance isn't the end of trust. It's the beginning of something more honest if you're willing to lead through it. **"**

- How can you turn resistance into a relational opportunity instead of a leadership obstacle?

Now write down one guiding question you want to carry with you the next time the work gets hard.

Because resistance isn't the end of trust. It's the beginning of something more honest if you're willing to lead through it.

CHAPTER 9

Stay Centered- Lead Without Losing Yourself

Somewhere between board meetings and bus duty, vision, and burnout, you might forget that you're human too.

You've made it through the noise, the politics, the patterns, and the pushback. But now comes something even harder:

Staying centered in a role designed to pull you in every direction.

The truth is, no one is immune to the toll of leadership. Even the most grounded leaders find themselves off balance. You pour into others all day—and some days, you come home empty.

So how do you keep leading with intention when the weight is heavy? How do you lead with heart without losing yourself? How do you stay grounded in your values when the job pulls you in a dozen directions?

This chapter is about the inner work—the kind that sustains you long after the honeymoon phase has ended.

Systems change is hard. People work is harder. But staying well while doing both? That's the real challenge... and the most important one.

Let's talk about what it looks like to lead with longevity, alignment, and soul.

The Center Doesn't Hold Itself

Leadership will stretch you—that's a given. But without practices that keep you centered, the stretch can become a downward spiral.

> Systems change is hard. People work is harder.

The most effective leaders aren't the ones who push through at all costs. They're the ones who know how to return to center when the weight pulls too hard.

Here are a few ways to protect your leadership and your well-being:

Create quiet margins. Even five minutes between meetings to breathe, walk, or reset your nervous system can change how you show up. If everything is back-to-back, your presence can't catch up with your position.

Define your non-negotiables. What are the things that keep you grounded—your family dinner time, your morning walk, journaling, prayer, therapy, yoga? Name them. Fiercely protect them. And for goodness sake...don't apologize for needing them!

Say no with purpose. Not every opportunity is aligned with your vision. Saying yes to everything dilutes your impact. Saying no, with clarity, helps you preserve energy for what matters most.

Process what's yours—and release what isn't. You'll absorb a lot in this role: frustration, grief, and projection. That doesn't mean you have to carry all of it. Get support. Journal. Talk it out. You can't be everyone's emotional landfill.

Stay tethered to your why. When the noise gets loud or the work feels blurry, return to your why. Keep it visible on your desk, your wall, your calendar. Let it re-anchor you on the days you want to walk away.

Build a trusted circle. Leadership can be isolating if you let it. You need a small group of colleagues you trust. These are the people who understand the weight of the role and can hold space when things get hard. For me, that's a group we call Powerhouse. We meet monthly to talk honestly, challenge each other's thinking, laugh, vent, and reconnect as humans, not just leaders.

Your well-being is not a luxury. It's not selfish. It's the strategy.

Burnout doesn't just take you out—it takes your impact with it.

Reflection Prompt: Staying Whole While Leading Hard

- Where in your life do you feel yourself getting stretched too thin?

- Is there a place you already know you need to set a boundary, but you just haven't said it out loud yet?

Write down one small habit that can serve as an anchor when everything else feels chaotic. Leadership doesn't require self-sacrifice. It requires self-awareness.

CHAPTER 10

The Work Begins Now

You've read the plan and heard the stories. You've started to think about what trust, culture, and connection really mean.

Now comes the part that can't be planned—only lived.

We don't master leadership by reading. It's lived—one hard decision, one honest conversation, one brave moment at a time.

And every day, you'll have choices to make:

Will you show up with presence, or just check the boxes?

Will you protect what's comfortable, or push for what's right?

Will you lead from fear or from who you actually are?

You won't find this work in the job descriptions, but it's the work that matters the most.

No one will hand you a roadmap for what's next. And that's okay.

You don't need a perfect plan.

You need to know what matters, and the guts to act on it.

And you've got those—or you wouldn't have made it this far!

The book may end here, but this is where the bold work of your leadership begins.

The kind of leadership that doesn't just maintain systems, but remakes them.

The kind of leadership that listens deeply, acts bravely, and centers people over politics.

The kind that refuses to be written by old rules.

You're not here to follow the path.

You're here to forge a new one.

Let's go.

A Closing Message

This book wasn't written to give you all the answers. It was written to remind you that you don't have to know it all—you just have to trust what's already in you!

The plan doesn't need to be perfect. You just need to begin with a courageous heart, the spirit of curiosity, and unrelenting conviction.

There will be days you doubt yourself. Return to these pages. There will be moments that test you. Revisit your why. And there will be breakthroughs, big and small, that remind you that this work matters. Because you matter.

Lead boldly. Lead human.

The next chapter isn't written yet.

You get to write it.

References

This book was shaped by the insights and research of many influential scholars and practitioners whose work has guided educational leadership for decades. Deep gratitude to the following thinkers whose ideas are referenced throughout the text:

Brown, B. (2018). Dare to lead: Brave work. Tough conversations. Whole hearts. Random House.

Deming, W. E. (2018). *Out of the Crisis*, reissue. MIT press.

Safir, S. (2017). The listening leader: Creating the conditions for equitable school transformation. Jossey-Bass.

Senge, P. M. (2006). The fifth discipline: The art and practice of the learning organization (Rev. ed.). Doubleday.

Watkins, M. (2003). The first 90 days: Critical success strategies for new leaders at all levels. Harvard Business School Press.

Meet the Author

Melanie Matta is a Superintendent/Principal, leadership practitioner, and founder of EdLeadership Lab with more than two decades of experience serving in small and rural school communities as a teacher, coach, principal, and district leader. Known for her human-centered approach, she focuses on building trust, strengthening systems, and supporting leaders as they step into roles that rarely come with a roadmap. She mentors emerging leaders, public speaker on practical leadership, and is pursuing her

doctorate in Educational Leadership with a focus on leadership transitions and superintendent retention in rural districts. *Unwritten: The Leadership Entry Plan No One Gave You—Until Now* is rooted in the real moments she has lived and witnessed, grounded in her belief that leadership is human work and that the first months in a new role can shape everything that follows.

FB: @melaniermatta @edleadershiplab

IG: @melaniermatta @edleadershiplab

www.ingramcontent.com/pod-product-compliance
Lightning Source LLC
Chambersburg PA
CBHW070643130626
46555CB00006B/2679